Inspired from Beyond

Library of Congress Control Number: 2018907101
ISBN: Hardcover   978-1-9845-3514-6
                Softcover   978-1-9845-3515-3
                eBook   978-1-9845-3516-0

Print information available on the last page.

Cover photo by Monica Redford at Onondaga Lake, Syracuse, NY

Rev. date: 06/23/2018

To order additional copies of this book, contact:
Xlibris
1-888-795-4274
www.Xlibris.com
Orders@Xlibris.com
780735

Inspired from Beyond

The Essence of a Past Love

Monica Redford and Dave

Introduction

This is a true memoir of a young romance and a metaphysical experience of connection after death. It shares love and happiness and the sorrow of never finding a way back together. The concept of love as being valid *until death do us part and in sickness and in health* does not necessarily have to be the only experience one can have. In matters of the heart, there is never any time limit on what love a heart can hold. Apparently, I had to learn a lesson that love is and always will be what really matters in a lifetime and in the afterlife. The experiences and people we meet cannot be taken for granted, as each of us is a teacher regardless of whether the experience is painful or joyful during our soul's journey.

Dedication

I dedicate this book to Michele Love, an Intuitive Medium at Healing Inspirations, a holistic healing and learning center. If her understanding of Twin Flames was not available, I never would have understood the dark painful years ahead. I also never would have known in which direction to look when I was searching for answers.

I also dedicate this book to my sisters, Kathy and Mary Kay, who may not have understood the unfamiliar choices I made but were a part of my finding the way.

Lastly, my children, Dava, Michael and Gina, who never criticized the journey I led during their growing up years and, instead, supported me with love and respect, truly the best gift a mother can receive.

"They are not dead who live in the hearts they leave behind." Tuscarora

This saying was taken from a Native book of Wisdom. There is no specific author, other than the nation listed.

There are so many quotes and inspirations to help us move on when we enter a space in time that we did not plan. People will encourage you with generic quotes or persuade you to move on when you encounter crises, sickness, personal setbacks or death, but sometimes you just have to go through the process of pain to understand the lesson. This is my story to share - an afterlife experience with a past love. I have said to the many skeptics, *"Just because you haven't experienced it – doesn't mean it can't exist."* The experience of grieving for someone after 50 years of not being in a relationship with that person was never dreamed of in my life's game plan. I have carried my story primarily alone, which made this journey so much harder to bear. Even so, it can never take away the experiences of genuine love I have had with others nor will I close the door to ever love again.

I love the quote by Brene Brown, *"When we deny our stories, they define us. When we tell our own our stories we get to write the ending."* I own this story, as painful as it is, as I will attempt to convey. I was never aware anything such as this could happen. The most traumatizing experience was the inability to share my daily struggles with others as I searched for a way to relieve my grief. When I tried to express my frustrations to others, I would always know my story was not being received, despite the person's kindness and politeness. Due to my emotional suffering, I began to write to release the confusion and pain I felt. If I use the word love when writing to this beloved, it is because I cannot find an appropriate word to convey my feelings. It has taken nearly four years for this short story to bring some understanding to print. And so my story begins.

After a second divorce, I kept myself busy with buying and restoring a few homes and then moved onto developing a small baking business along with my full time job as a secretary. These roles could not erase the solitude I felt, along with frustration and loneliness at times. I questioned my attractiveness and the reasons for the failure of my marriages. During that time, I truly wanted a person in my life, but the idea of using the Internet for dating was not right for me. When I did try the Internet for a brief few months, it confirmed what I believed — that this means of meeting someone would not help me sense the chemistry I needed in selecting a person. I continued keeping busy with the hope someone would just walk into my life.

Years passed with my children's weddings, grandchildren being born and many house moves due to an unsettling within myself. Few real vacations to relax and enjoy were ever taken. I looked forward to family visits with children, who lived at a distance, but never quite got the type of experience I enjoyed hearing from family and friends who vacationed. During those years, with every day work as a secretary and home maker, I found an interest in metaphysical philosophies and became a Reiki and Karuna Master. I didn't realize I would face much uncertainty with a forced retirement or how much spirituality and holistic healing would be needed to help me move on. I practiced Reiki as a volunteer at a local hospital, work which may have helped me more than the patients. I also did a lot of work on myself to heal and took my soul's journey seriously. The anger over the unexpected early retirement with no financial back up plan caused incredible confusion and loss, monetarily and emotionally. Then, having an elderly father living with me was another filling up of time and space, quickly eating up the years that were now passing me by.

In the summer of 2014, I attended a class on Twin Flames or Souls taught by Michele Love at Healing Inspirations. I didn't find it necessary to worry or seek my Twin Flame but chose to do one of her suggestions. She asked the class to write a letter to their Twin Flame angel. Everyone has an angel and, yes, I always believed that, but this idea seemed a bit off, and I skeptically questioned why this was necessary. I wrote a note to this newly named angel, tossed it in a drawer and forgot about it until much later. The note said: Dear Angel of Twin Flame, I need someone to share my life who has the same values, goals, interests and, especially, who fits in with my family. Please, before the end of the year, send someone who is waiting for me.

By the end of November, I received the sad news that an ex-boyfriend of almost 45 years ago, Dave, had passed. It shook me, yet I couldn't anticipate the raw emotions that would follow. While rearranging a drawer, I rediscovered my angel letter before the end of the year. Without even considering that his death may have been an answer to the angel request, I wept uncontrollably without knowing why. When I reflect on my reaction to hearing of his death and my experience at the wake and funeral, my emotions seem extreme for someone who had not been in a relationship with Dave for decades. This was before I started writing and spending so much time and money to learn how and why something like this could happen.

An explanation of Twin Flames or Twin Souls (not to be confused with soul mates): where one soul splits into two before they come to earth. One soul gravitates more toward spiritual existence and the other toward material existence. I did not completely buy this theory. I never heard of it before the class, but apparently there are many people who have experienced this and are compelled to write or speak about it. As people are becoming enlightened in their spirituality, they are waking up to understandings that — although they were not taught these truths earlier — have been around since the beginning of time. These enlightened people are usually sensitive and will pick up on things other people take for granted. A lesson on Twin Flame (www.TwinFlame.com) reads:

Being on the Twin Flame journey does not mean you need to be in a relationship with someone, it merely requires you to be in a relationship with yourself, to become strong, devotional and on purpose; to seek out your short comings and rise above all shadow and darker aspects of your soul so that a harmonization occurs. We become balanced and whole in ourselves and each other. Why can't they find each other? There is some disconnectedness, some veil that keeps them separated yet they are so close.

Though we may not understand why we have separated, there is a reason that is higher than ourselves that is helping us to learn lessons on earth such as detachment, forgiveness, surrender, inner strength and trust. Twin Flame is not a pleasant ordeal and will leave one with a string of questions in your head with no real answers. The interesting part is you never feel disconnected.

Elizabeth Gilbert writes, *"People think a soul mate is your perfect fit and that's what everyone wants. But a true soul mate is a mirror, the person who shows you everything that is holding you back, the person who brings you to your own attention so you can change your life."*

Most metaphysical experts in this understanding with whom I met feel my experience is Twin Flame. I really don't care how one defines it, but — based on the research I have done — I most definitely have experienced the separation, pain and grief that fits the description when one soul departs.

Sitting at a restaurant, a week before Thanksgiving of 2014, a former classmate informed me of Dave's passing. My feelings were of shock and then sadness. I questioned people, but no one knew what had happened. I knew I would learn more at his wake.

It wasn't until the wake, I learned of his health issues. As I approached the casket, I struggled to view him, a man who looked nothing like the man I remembered. Dave was a caregiver type of individual who chose to sacrifice his own well-being for others. He was often warned that he was gambling with his own life. He was encouraged to get the open heart surgery that his body was visibly telling him was needed. I learned later he was putting his partner first and didn't know how he could balance recovery from an operation for himself and caregiving. He went to the doctor's office one November day and had a heart attack then admitted to the hospital. The family told me there was nothing the doctors could do to save him. Over the years, I was not aware this man was not taking good care of his own life. Although I used to think that eventually I would bump into him somewhere in town, I never felt the urgency to force it.

I would meet his children in the receiving line at the wake for the first time. I was asked by his adult daughter and son how I knew their father. I said, "I went to school with him." They asked my name and when I told them Monica they immediately replied, "Our Dad spoke of you." I was flattered yet surprised, wondering when would he have spoken of me. Kiddingly, I asked if they heard the story about the driving lesson. They laughed and said, "Yes, he told us."

The driving lesson experience: Over the years, regardless of what stage of my life I was in, I had the odd experience of bursting into laughter whenever the memory crossed my mind of an evening when Dave and I double dated with my sister and her husband. The memory of one particular night always stuck with me. Dave had a new red convertible and allowed me to drive it. I took the wheel with no fear. As we were rounding a corner, I let the steering wheel slip through my fingers and the car ended up sideways on a sloped hill in our village. The car was at a tilt with the ability to roll. When I turned around, Kathy and Mike were thrown to one side of the car unable to get out due to the angle we were in. Dave jumped into action and somehow managed to help us out of the car with the help of Mike and someone who heard the racket and came running to assist in moving the car safely off the hill.

Dave asked, "What were you thinking while steering the car?" I replied, I thought I saw on TV you can let the wheel spin through your fingers and for some reason instead of gripping the wheel tightly I let it slide through my fingers. Dave's reaction was priceless. It made the memory ten times more enjoyable. In my reflecting on this, it was my private moment of a sick sense of humor but it always made me smile. He was patient and kind to me always, but I don't recall ever getting a driving lesson again. Now, since his passing, I never am amused by this as I had been over the decades.

When I viewed the series of pictures of Dave's life at the funeral home, I was taken aback. All of a sudden, I was asking myself, "How did I forget the essence of him?" I understood there would be some nostalgia, but this was different and I questioned, "Why am I feeling this way?"

I met a sister of his, and she said his body could not withstand the heart attack and possibly, even if he had lived, he might not have been the same. She questioned where he would have been able to live if he had recovered. I did all I could to stop myself from saying, "But I would have taken him in." This was the second time in my memory I questioned something about us out of the blue that did not logically make sense to question. I was more caught up with questioning why I felt this desire to help when nothing had happened between us for so many years. It was just an inner awareness. I also didn't question why she made such a comment. Why wouldn't he have gone back to the woman with whom he was living?

The following day I went to the funeral. The priest spoke of Dave's acts of kindness throughout his life. At communion, I walked by the casket and touched it as my last good bye. Before the final moments at the mass's end, the tears came flooding down my cheeks. I left quickly. Without understanding why, I would continue to cry for many days. Then, days turned into months and then years. I was shocked that I was so overwhelmed and could not process what was happening.

To find some peace, I was inspired to write a post as a tribute on a Face Book prayer circle referring to my thoughts after the wake. I wrote:

"I know these words may be confusing but I am just expressing loss. Tonight I visited the wake of a beloved from years ago. It was one of those moments when you wondered what if, I should have seen him one more time, the memories, his wonderful family and a slew of thoughts that made you realize he was a small part of what became part of me. I realized as I said words to him tonight, the prayer for his family and the knowledge he was home in heaven before his body ever released him was comfort. Dave was a part of my life given-taken and now embracing it for what was. Peace and Comfort"

I did not know his daughter was on that website and the next morning there was a comment thanking me for my post. She wrote, "My Dad always spoke so fondly of you." I was sad reading this because I wondered how he went through life not contacting me or anyone else when I was alone for so long.

Dave's death was just before the Christmas holidays of 2014. Instead of my mourning subsiding, it became a part of my daily life, so I returned to Healing Inspirations, a wonderful shop practicing metaphysical helps that I was so blessed to have found. I went to a message circle with Michele Love. A message circle is where a medium has a psychic gift to share a message that is needed for each person and sometimes from a past loved one from the beyond. After the message circle, I asked Michele, who taught the Twin Souls/Flames class I had attended before, if she understood why I was experiencing this deep grief. I sincerely never connected this experience with her class on Twin Flame. She said, "Meet your Twin Flame. Dave will be around you forever." I told her some practitioners told me just throw this grief to the universe and move forward. They said you should let go of anything that doesn't serve you anymore. She laughed and said I could not discard or toss to the universe what I have as we have always been together as souls.

Everything Michele said was comforting, and I went home to check sources about Twin Souls on the Internet. It was quite amazing to read the stories of people who met their twin. Unfortunately for those who had a twin who passed over, it described the one left behind experiencing physical, mental and emotional pain. The only stories I resonated with were the ones when the other person died. The term *excruciating pain* was used. Those were the exact words I would use to describe my life at that time. I do not want to be repetitive in my writing, but this desire to revisit my past and reconnect with Dave had become a daily emotional roller coaster that just brought no relief. These emotions would bring me to contact mediums and others to reduce the pain and intense grief I felt.

From a portion of Ashley Davis Bush's LCSW Grief Has No Closure from Psychology Today:

"We live in a culture that avoids emotional discomfort. In fact, our society makes it easy to look for distractions and diversions from all things painful. If we can drink, eat, shop, play or Facebook grief away, we will.

But here's the truth — losing a loved one is excruciatingly painful. And it doesn't just hurt for a few days, a few weeks, a few months, or even a few years. The impact of a major loss is lifelong. Emotional "closure" is a cultural myth.

Why? Because no matter how many years go by — 10, 20, 30 — you will be changed irrevocably. You may think of your dear one almost daily and you will have days out of the blue that knock the wind right out of you. Certainly, the pain softens and eases over time. However, normal grief will always have moments of reoccurring sharpness, pain as raw as the very first day."

The best day dreams of him are a waste. They cannot be lived out. When I see him in the dream, it's too hard to bear that he is so far away from my everyday life. Yes, it could be delusion. It could be a message. It could be a test. Whatever this is I can't stop putting myself under a microscope to understand why and what is happening to me. I quickly learned that blocking this grief would create more pain.

Without getting too detailed, in 2014 before his death, for the first time in 45 years, I had a strong urge to contact him. That year, I took up bowling after many years of not participating. I was pretty rusty and I remember thinking if only I could call him and ask him to show me how to throw the curve. Dave was a PBA bowler and who better to teach me his follow through, which worked so well. I would actually throw the ball and, as I walked back, visualize him watching me. I chose not to search him out, as I believed he was in a relationship and it just seemed selfish and inappropriate. I also never called him because the makeshift curve I tossed threw my side out. I needed several chiropractor appointments and never bowled again.

During that year I dated a guy for a few months — someone I should have dropped after the first date but didn't because I questioned whether I was being too particular. I'd run into a friend of Dave's, one of his golf buddies, at a local restaurant from time to time. I often wanted to ask where they played so I could innocently show up. But the semi-commitment dating trial kept me from pursuing my curiosity. There is something that haunts me about this golf buddy. He wanted to date me, and I always used the guy I was dating infrequently as an excuse to put him off. I did not put it past this person to brag to Dave that he was waiting to go out with me. He would randomly say negative things about Dave, which I thought odd. It may be my ego, but knowing Dave as I did, it would have been unlike him not to have said, "Tell

Mon I said, 'Hi'." After the death, I asked this person if I ever came up in conversation and he said no. My gut said differently, that he was lying. It did come up during a medium reading that Dave absolutely was sending a message and I never got it. This particular person has not owned this, and whether it is true or not, I always regret that my life was so complicated at the time that I did not send Dave a message. These two situations give me such regret regardless of my questioning whether it would have been the ethical thing to do.

I soon learned that friends and family were not the people to seek out in this situation. I learned to hold it in until I could make an appointment to process the feelings with a counselor or a medium. Initially, I was so overwhelmed, I tried at times to find comfort talking with anyone who knew him. One person's response was, "Would you just let Dave die in peace?" The most painful voice of those trying to help me was, "You need to get over it – move on." Get over what? These comments were for them not me. I would not intentionally put myself into this mental state, as I was not being fed anything about him physically or emotionally to encourage the thoughts. I had no idea how I could be in so much pain over someone I hadn't seen for decades. My life was busy enough, but this was new and it would take time and money before I could find peace.

Why does this come back to haunt me? As I learned after months, the relationship he was in at the time of his death was not the healthiest for his easy going personality. I also learned he was talking about leaving his last relationship and was being threatened by his partner if he went through with it. Knowing this only increased my frustration. Why didn't I know this before? As in many stories of Twin Flames, this is exactly how it plays out. Lives of Twin Flames can run parallel where they know there is absence of something but they do not know what it actually is. I honestly would say to myself over the years and before his death that it seems someone is supposed to call me but isn't following through. I cannot express how many times this notion of someone not calling me went through my mind. Oddly enough, since his passing, I never wonder who isn't calling or ask that question.

One of the mediums shared that Dave is now aware of our soul connection and understands the reason for our separation. He doesn't want me to stay in this painful state but instead wants me to be brought back to my authentic self as he knew me in our innocence and happiness. I am hoping to give back to him his very request as I work on myself daily.

The emotional reaction I lived each day did not make sense. I could not get him out of my head. I felt like I was a part of his family. I tried to be sensitive when contacting his family members, who were kind and seemed interested in what I was experiencing at first. Right about the same time, all three contacts – his sister, his niece and his friend would not return my calls. I asked for very little information and most definitely stayed away from asking for anything personal. They questioned why I did not contact him before this time seeming to hint at blame. I tried to explain that to my knowledge Dave was in a relationship and I would not entertain intruding. Oddly enough, I had a medium come to my home and as soon as she walked into the room knowing absolutely nothing of this asked if "passive/aggressive" meant anything to me. I answered, "No." She asked again later. At the end of the session I shared my frustration of being shut out by family.

She immediately said that was the passive/aggressiveness she sensed. Her background in psychology helped her understand how vulnerable I was, having shared my pain with the family but then being left with their lack of empathy in understanding why was I experiencing such a heavy heart over Dave's death. For myself, if this was in reverse, I most definitely would want to know how a person experiencing such grief was doing from time to time. If he were alive, Dave most definitely would want to know how the person grieving was doing. That is just my personal belief.

Years before his death, I heard his mother was in the hospital so I stopped by to visit. It was wonderful anytime I saw her, but because of Dave's marriage I didn't always feel it was right to drop in as many times as she came to mind or as many times as I wanted to. It would be the last time I ever heard her say, "I wish you were my daughter-in-law." I asked if I could pray with her before I left, and we did. Within a day or two I heard she had passed on. One of the psychics I later met guessed her name and said she had been with me many lifetimes before. I wasn't sure whether to believe that but was amazed the psychic immediately guessed her name.

I saw Dave only two times, in 45 years. The first time was when visiting his new born baby, and the second at his mother's wake. I often thought about his mother's wake, as he stood in line staring and smiling at me standing in the back. I can re-live that moment as if it was yesterday, as it seemed he was trying to connect with me. I do not recall what I said to him in the receiving line but I do remember his saying, "You're still beautiful." I didn't think too much about it meaning anything because I had heard that after his divorce he was with a woman much older than us. I thought, back then in my late 40's, that his being involved with someone so very much older was strange.

Before this event, my understanding of death was that it was final with no more communication or relationship with the departed. His death, though, brought a barrage of memories, thoughts of him so vivid, remembrance of good and bad times, sounds and funny expressions he made. People would ask, if this was the love of your life or your soul mate then why didn't the two of you stay together? I will need to go back to our initial meeting and dating experience to answer that.

The relationship began in my senior year of high school when I passed a classroom and heard a guy yell out, "Wait, who is she!?" It is so strange that I still remember the A-line green paisley dress my mother made that I was wearing. It was a good and modern look for the time. We later exchanged greetings and he asked me out. Our dating made going to high school fun and exciting. It was a very fast connection and romance, which really stepped up my interest in being in school every day. Our personalities were pretty opposite. I was a shy, naïve girl. He was an extrovert and had no problem fitting into any situation. Our being opposite temperaments helped me feel better about myself while coming out of the awkward years. My biggest challenge with him was that he was flirtatious, or at least that is how I viewed him back then. He was not threatening our relationship. I was not accustomed to so much high energy. I was more unsure of myself and, most likely, any long term relationship or marriage would not have worked. I say this because many people back in the late 60's were getting married after high school or college.

I do recall a lot of playful arguing and making up. He was so confident and cheerful and always raised himself above the bar in helping others. I looked up to him, but I was not grounded enough to see a lifetime together. He was the guy in the red convertible, preferably wanting the top down and always picking me up with the top down until I whined enough that he put it back up. I had that long straight flipped hair with heavy bangs like Marlo Thomas on the TV series "That Girl", which was the style in those years. He had an infectious smile and was always free as a bird, laughing and never a care in the world. When I think about it now, he truly lived in the moment and enjoyed life.

To understand my love for Dave you need to know a little bit more about him. He was the son of a business owner in our small town. His mother absolutely adored me, and I really liked her. My mother very much accepted him and appreciated his respect for me. He had one brother and three sisters, and they were a pretty lively bunch. I recall our typical dates, which consisted of drive-in movies, bowling, dinners, Vernon Downs horse races and car racing. He really knew how to treat a girl, and entertainment was always a part of the date. I found newspaper clippings of our friends' weddings. We actually stood up for three different weddings together. I have tried to retrace other significant events. If we had been allowed one more talk about our past, it would have given me so many more memories and answered so many more questions. I recall the dozen beautiful yellow roses, the very large bottle of Shalimar perfume and the most precious Valentine gift I ever received or even remember being given by anyone – a bowling ball with my initials. The beautiful yellow roses have come up in several medium readings.

I cannot remember how we parted. I know it was the era of the Vietnam War. He joined the Navy, as opposed to being drafted. I'll always remember visiting him in Norfolk, VA and our walk at the ocean. On his weekend leaves, he would drive home to Syracuse from Virginia to see me. When I think back, he did it so effortlessly, but we were young and in love and so glad to be together. At some point, though, we parted ways. I believe it was me who ended the relationship. I found dating long distance extremely hard, and it was just easier "out of sight – out of mind." I believe that in those early years we were both destined to paths that would keep us apart forever. It is so odd to me that this mental practice of shutting someone out of mind does not work now, especially after death.

I found interest in my faith, but I became overzealous. I joined the Jesuit Volunteer Corps and was sent to the South Pacific and Oregon. My initial intention was good, but through the encouragement of very conservative Christians back home — not the Jesuits — instead of enjoying my life and my faith, I became very rigid and conservative. Books and tapes that were mailed to me and that I read diligently, had a further hardening effect on me. Little did I know this would take years to undo. The letter of the law would be easier for me to live by than exercising my heart and trusting my God-given intuition.

When I returned home two years later, Dave was married. Oddly enough, I do remember thinking, "He couldn't wait." Now there was no reason for me to have thought this. We did not have a plan. It was just an odd thought that I never forgot. A few years later I married. My husband and I visited his wife and him to bring a baby gift. I've asked myself why we did this and what prompted this? I think it was visiting his mother and learning of their child's birth that made me comfortable enough to contact them for a quick welcome, and Dave and my husband did know each other, so it wasn't too odd. Unfortunately, the one thing I will never forget was how quiet and subdued he was. That is sad for me to remember but, for him, it was the beginning of a change that would eventually be a precursor to his future.

I am beginning to wonder now about an experience in my first marriage from which I could not seem to find my way back and which resulted in my husband and I separating. Someone whose path I crossed had a temperament and personality like Dave's and so reminded me of him. I became addicted to him and he literally filled a void. I wouldn't think of breaking up Dave's marriage, but my marriage was totally destroyed. At the time, I did not know it was an addiction and that I still loved my husband; but without guidance as to what was happening and without understanding, I was about to enter a very dark period. This was a time in my life when, again, I was in a religion that was pretty black and white. I would act, think and live each day dying to self. I had a narrow view on life except for what I heard from the pulpit, and it became my toxic faith. This is another story to be written.

Getting out of the fundamental religion seemed to be a slow but steady withdrawal from the false sense of high I had lived. I once again felt alive and felt feelings and energy that I had shut off. I did not want to return to the closed mental and spiritual world I had built from fundamental teachings. As a result, my marriage was ending because I couldn't seem to separate the two. As hard as I prayed for forgiveness and sought help and deliverance, I needed to go forward, a journey which would become one of loss and sorrow.

I contacted a medium long distance. She said many things that convinced me Dave and I still have a connection and that we were not mature enough when we were teenagers to have had a successful lasting relationship. She said it might be too early to really hear from him from the other side but advised me to practice meditations. Messages are received and given telepathically. Her reading saw me in a life lesson but she told me not to spend all my time beating myself up for missing my opportunity while he was living. What I was experiencing was necessary. She encouraged me to remain open to what he brings. In response to this, three years later I can only say I truly try daily to live in the moment. There is a never ending awareness though that something is missing and that awareness brings him to the forefront. This grief has never stopped the momentum in my life, and I am doing everything I need to do. I could never use it as an excuse for not handling living day to day. I live to the fullest, aware of loss.

I also went to a counsellor at a local Bereavement Center. The counsellor was very interested in this story and sympathetic. She said, "This type of grieving would be harder to work through and may take longer than usual. It is not just his death but the experiences and opportunities over the many years you will grieve." She said she speaks to her husband whom she lost years before every day and I would feel better if I did same. As a priest told me, "This person must have thought a great deal of you to have his presence in your life this strong. Be sure to talk to him often."

I know my emphasis throughout my story is on pain and confusion, but this is not like a headache or toothache where you understand where the pain is stemming from. The problem is the grief is so deep. It lets up for a while and then crashes down. I have said the best prayers I have ever verbalized in my life. Michele Love once explained that grief is as if a part of your physical body has been removed. If all of a sudden you became an amputee, you would need to learn how to live without a leg or an arm. This analogy might be the closest to explaining a missing piece of me. I have had questions that should be answered by now — especially, what do I do with this experience and will someone just make this pain go away? This suffering intensified during hard times in my life but I always knew the difference from daily trials I was experiencing day to day and his crossing over.

I visited Coleen Shaugnessy, famous for her psychic and angel readings. She said she would know instantly if this was a Twin Flame or just a past love. She was very excited and said this is a connection for all time. She told me that this was not the first time we had been together. Her advice was that maybe this was too early for me to hear from him as the other medium had said. Meditating at that time was more painful then helpful. In time, meditation would be a time to look forward to. She asked me to trust my instincts, which most definitely would take more time.

A year later another medium saw three old Italian women dressed in black from head to toe, veil and all. She and I did not understand what this meant. It was much later that I learned both Dave and my ancestors were from the same area of Italy. Our grandfathers were from northern Italy or of Tyrol descent and from the same valley of Val de Chiese - Giudicarie. On our mothers' side, both families lived around Naples originally. I never knew his background. This may be why I blurted out once to his sister, "I feel so close to you. I feel like we are family." Over 45 years ago, I had very little contact with his younger sister as we were in our late teens when we dated and she was so much younger than me.

Another medium, Barbara Bennett, clairvoyantly saw Dave enter the room with me and stand behind me. Without knowing my concerns, she asked if my husband had passed. She surmised a strong commitment to spirituality that drew him to me. During the course of our session, Dave told her he felt responsible for missing opportunities to find me. She said this was a soul commitment we made but she was not sure how to fix it. This wouldn't be the last time I heard that we had many lifetimes together, but his life ended in a way no one would have anticipated. Dave's work on earth was done. My work was far from done. The medium's spiritual guides told her, though she had never heard of this type of encounter, that I was not faking my story. Dave said, "I don't want her to cry all the time for me." Mutually, he will be watching me from afar sending love and prayers, an old soul looking after you. Barbara said, "He wants you to enjoy the rest of your time here." He felt his male ego got in his way and to forgive him. I told her, "I did forgive him. I can't forgive myself right now." She said it's unusual for those who passed over to admit any fault, but that was not the last time I was to hear regret from him. I often am reminded that if I was not so invested in my spirituality, this experience may have gone unnoticed and been interpreted as something else that could have led me to a serious depression.

Barbara felt this is a situation where two souls promised to be together and didn't. Again this is typical of a Twin Flame. She looked at his picture and noted his "honest eyes." She told me he feels we missed a lot of moments because of him and missed the love and nurturing we both needed. He wishes he could fix the pain but he will always be around. She encouraged me to talk to him and said he will answer in different ways. He is trying to apologize for not finding me and there is regret. The one thing she felt he strongly conveyed was his appreciation for my understanding him. As for me, I feel I understand him more now than I ever did in the past.

1ˢᵗ letter to Dave

How did I miss you? You were everywhere tonight in my mind. You were the 60's guy. I feel so sad knowing I have to ride this out with never a chance to run into you – never – so my imagination sees you as you were. It remembers our favorite pizza spot splitting half a large pizza and our not having any problem devouring it, the looks you gave me and that wink, the infectious smile, the cool dresser you were. I miss you and haven't seen you in decades. It's not fair. I've wanted for so long to connect with someone that gets me. Pray for me as I for you. Love, Mon

2ⁿᵈ letter to Dave

I wish we didn't meet in the 60's. I am forever searching to find a way to live with this. I made multiple mistakes, experienced much heartache and then faced your passing.

Ten months and it is still unclear how you came into my mind and heart so clearly. A day without remorse, grief and sadness would be nice but not so. I can't go back. You can't come back. All chances gone - only questions left unanswered. Love, Mon

3r letter to Dave - Not sure how to pray but sending you 'love and prayers'. My little money being spent to practitioners to ease the pain emotionally and to see if there is a message from beyond. You were not phony. You changed from everything I feared and became something I never would have wanted to happen to you. The women seemed domineering in your life and that changed the man I once knew. Your pain I inherited after you passed. I feel hopeless at times. I lived with anxiety from a loss that cannot be recovered. Desires that burn deeply as I cannot stop the yearning to have you show up. There are places, music and memories that bring in such nostalgia that I am not blind to. I keep busy and involved to keep my sanity. Love, Mon

Dear Dave,

I have few memories yet it's hard not to push a good memory away. Sometimes it's just being near your old family home that pulls me in. Regardless of the pain and sadness remembering our few years is a comfort knowing I once had you and now in a different realm you are still around. Our lives seemed to be so busy over the past decades. From what little I learned, you were the one who served the relationship you were in and someone else was being waited on. You took little care for yourself and your partner who seems to have depended on you or co-depended on you did not encourage your attending to your physical needs as one would expect in a relationship.

I spoke with a friend of yours the year prior to your death and though I don't think it was malicious, she did not tell me how unhappy you were. I do not know why she kept this from me when she and I were having a discussion about relationships and lack of mine prior to your passing. Yet at the wake she felt it important to state, "I always thought you two would get back together." She was not the only one to state this and again another person who knew of my aloneness said nothing till you were gone. So it is odd people knew our conditions were far from happy and no one said anything to encourage us to arrange a meeting. I don't accept the saying "It's God's will," in this situation. I think this story holds substance because it is so unbelievable one would feel this much pain and truly feel such deep grief losing you. Love, Mon

I don't know if I first saw it on Facebook or in my looking up information on the Internet. I came across a retired private investigator who actually researched death after the passing of his father. His program has famous people, doctors and near death experience survivors - just an incredibly interesting cast that would tell their experiences. I tuned in because I was fascinated with learning something I had no knowledge of before. The program is <u>Afterlife TV </u>with Bob Olson. Hearing of people who died and then came back to life changed my understanding of life after death and took any fear out of dying.

As indicated before, with Twin Souls there is no such thing as closure. They existed before and will exist forever. There is nothing to close this experience. When I researched the experiences of Twin Flames or Souls, I learned that among those whose partner passed, the one left behind entered a very dark and "excruciating pain." That term was used over and over again from the testimonies I heard. I spoke with a woman who had this experience for 18 years even after her marriage. I told her I do not have 18 years left. Oddly enough, one night flipping channels I saw a portion of the *Twilight* series. When Bella had thought she lost Edward there was a scene where she woke at night screaming. I never woke at night screaming, but I woke many nights keeled over in emotional pain and in grief that I could not stop the pain and the crying.

I am not sure, but this experience is conveying a feeling my existence has been altered. There is an awareness more than I ever felt before that something is missing in my life. I can't deny what I am experiencing. When I am focused and doing a project I am totally into it pushing – pushing myself all the time. It's not normal. This shouldn't be happening. I am caught in deep grief. I am a survivor and cannot play the victim role. When I am through with the project or work, the tears are released in relief. Some might think, maybe she is lonely and made up this fantasy. Those statements could only be made by people who do not know me. There are millions of men out in the world, and as one of my best friends has said for years, "You could have anyone but you will never just have anyone."

I questioned his choice of partners over the years. What attracted them to each other? How? When? Was it ever life giving? How long before he became a servant and stopped caring for himself? When did the partnership stop being, or was she ever someone he fell in love with? What kept him from asking and accepting advice? These are questions I hoped the family would share with me. I think it would have been kind of them to help me process by accepting a couple of calls but they didn't owe it to me to keep the conversation going. It was easy to see they felt sorry for me or could not really understand an old partner's death having such a deep impact, when so little time had been spent together. Due to this lack of communication with his family, I realize I cannot convey in my story so much of what I don't remember or know about him. I couldn't even get a photo of the two of us, which I requested. There had to be a spiritual connection that is not defined by our earthly walk as we know it. If nothing else, we most definitely were a part of a soul family from years past.

Several months later a member of the family asked me had I been seeing Dave before his death. I emphatically said, "No. I wish I could say differently." I know they must have been talking and felt something had been going on but that is not so. I know it seemed impossible to believe that I could be in such sadness, and it might have seemed that I was lying. I understand the family might not have delved into any possibilities on the spiritual level. Logically, it did not add up. I often prayed, "Why couldn't we have one meeting that would have eliminated this happening to me?" One meeting at least I could look back on and say, no we weren't interested or yes let's find a way. I find no gratification in using this process for losses that have occurred in my life. As I wrote earlier, I always was an out of sight, out of mind individual. Psychologically, this does not equate to who I always have been.

Being so torn and trying to accept this closure was an everyday battle. I put myself down and I regretted that I ever spoke about it to anyone outside metaphysical understanding. Regardless of being extremely selective about individuals with whom I would share, the person I confided in would just go silent. I felt people thought I was crazy. A metaphysical friend and life coach, Denise McKee, sympathized with my pain but reminded me of what she remembered before this incident. Denise explained, "Look at what you went through over the past couple of years before he passed: adjusting to the loss of a job, a botched up surgery, the role of caregiver, finances, etc. You are too hard on yourself. Dave also may have been so involved in the situation he was in and questioning how he could leave the partner he lived with." Over the past years, Dave and I were looking at our problems, and the negativity we faced was overwhelming. There was little creative energy left to look beyond our problems. I speak for him based on what I learned from his loved ones resonating with the mediums' words

A note to self:

Nothing much has changed. The world is heavier. The world seems off, knowing he is not here. I have him floating in and out all the time in my mind. When I am alone it is the worst. No one can explain the tremendous flood of tears that flow - the words, the thoughts and the grief that grips me so deeply. I cannot help trying to resolve this and make the pain go away because it is affecting my everyday life.

I frequent the gravesite at least twice a month. It is where I want to go and talk regardless of all the talking and praying I normally do. I know he is not there; but as I have read in articles on death, his spirit may have been a passenger in the car as I drove there. I change the arrangements in the vases according to the season and find this gratifying

With Twin Souls there is an undeniable unconditional love regardless of their history, any hurt or broken promises. This unconditional understanding of another regardless of faults, sin and imperfection is key to me. I can honestly assert that nothing can be said to break my love and belief. My friend Len had a message from her mother after she passed. The message was, "Tell Len life goes on." She encouraged me that a Twin Flame is very real as the souls are one. She encouraged me to be gentle with myself and that he truly hears my words and is near.

Christmas 2014 - the holiday he planned on leaving his living situation

To Dave's wonderful family, (written in a Christmas card)

His leaving has brought unexpected grief to me. I have spent the last 20 years alone feeling the only thing I can do is look back and be thankful I even had a relationship with Dave in my youth. We were very young but he definitely left such an impression on me. I know when I was younger I feared our differences and it scared me off. I see now his dedication, generosity and selflessness were something any woman would desire. I will not accept a relationship that shows no respect and respect is definitely what he gave me. For now, I spend time talking with him, visits to the cemetery and crying in prayer asking why couldn't I have run into him at least once when we could have taken a second look. As a friend put it, in those days, life was easier and carefree. We did not have the burdens we carry today. I was happy but after two divorces I have been so unhappy for far too long. I did not know his circumstances but it would have been totally inappropriate to contact him anyways in his relationship.

Your family is so beautiful. Thank you for always being kind to me when it could have been so easy to ignore me. I know that angels were there when no else was on that fateful day. Love, Monica

A letter to Dave:

This has been another tearful week. I can't believe how I feel so much loss when you come to mind. I am not trying to punish myself with these thoughts. They are just made so real by the emotional pain I carry day after day. I am trying to force myself to listen to the music I am most moved by. They are the songs of our era. It always put me right with you then, and now it does the same. The difference is I can't stop crying when hearing it now so I have refrained from listening to the music. I would say the best song (and there are many) that describes this is Kenny Rogers and Gladys Knight "If We Knew Then What We Know Now." Back in the day, I would daydream and be anxious for your call or visit. I am asking you to send me someone in the interim. I am so unhappy. I listen to people who write their stories of true love, and people who find their partners from the past and start again. I did not have that with you. I didn't even get close to that, though I know you always wanted us to marry young. I love you Dave – I miss your smile, your funny ways, and just the physical companionship I need so much now. I'm writing this from a class I am taking in Creative Writing. I question why anyone would want to read of someone's torment when I don't have enough answers why this is happening to me. The desires will be coming out more and more in my writing because they are ever there. Love, Mon

The past year, a local professional bowler friend of Dave, much older than he was, passed away. I read the obituary and felt anger and sadness that Dave died so young and went first. That day was extremely painful. I couldn't shake the heaviness and cried a lot. It felt like I fell in a hole. Plans to go out were cancelled. I would never know when to expect the highs and lows of grief. The next day was better but I think the obituary triggered the anger of Dave passing too soon.

Later the next year I took on a temp job at the USBC (Bowling Congress) registering bowlers from around the world. It was a very powerful experience because it was like Dave was everywhere. I can see if he had never died we surely would have met there. The work was fast and involved, so I was extremely focused. Leaving to drive home, though, brought out all the emotions. Dave said to the last medium he believed the experience brought us full circle.

During these years I lived daily in pain trying to let go. This was a typical prayer to be delivered from the agony.

A letter to Archangel Azrael, the angel for those crossing over and those grieving: I am of sound mind. I am in love. I am trying to understand how to survive. Where are you? So much has been put on me to survive and pull myself together. Where is the benefit and when does the grieving become peaceful? I pray for Dave as he obviously had more to gain by leaving. Regardless I remember our interests and our playfulness. How does it resolve itself inside me? With all my communication to him, how can I be sure he cares what I feel or say? It's like this was the meanest trick anyone could ever play. I feel like the woman waiting on the shore for the sailor to come home but he never appears. Is this some joke? A meeting in a neutral place would have prevented all of this. But there was no meeting. No wonder his mother longed for our getting together. Who thought like this back then? It was like she was psychic.

I've done so much work on myself yet I learned a life lesson that creates heart shock, pain, and loss from the past.

Lesson: We all experience voids in our life from time to time. This void in me is so real. I cannot find any experience — social interactions, food, or person — to fill the emptiness. I hate it. I do not live in the past but reminders are comforting and at the same time can be incredibly painful. Understanding the spirit world is necessary, and it is unfortunate we are not better prepared to face loss when it happens. I have been a regular church going person all my life but feel the teaching of death can be too ambiguous. I know there are certain spiritual passages, rites, resurrection, reincarnation or whatever you subscribe to, but death and grief are not taught enough. My hope is that through this writing I will help someone who faces this experience to embrace the loss and be open.

I have my 1968 yearbook and have read his short comment at different times over the years and honestly could not bring up any feeling. After his death, I picked it up one day and read it as I had many times before. It had an impact on me that I was not anticipating. I completely fell apart and was afraid to read it again for another year.

It read: *Monica, To a wonderful and beautiful girl. You are the kind of girl I can't live without for too long. I will never forget the way we met and our first date. See you around and good luck in the future with "Dave." May God Bless You. Dave P.S. I Love You.*

This certainly is not a love sonnet or poetry, but something about his feelings, his penmanship, an innocent space in time so many years ago now spoke to me clearly.

Since I have spent a good amount of time over the years working on myself, I question why I was given this experience when it could have been given to someone else who has never worked on themselves. Well maybe because I would be just that type of person to delve into this and not let go until I have answers and can put this to rest by writing my story. A local author who inspired me with her journey over the loss of her husband is Anne Marie Higgins. In her book, *Dancing in Two Realms, A Love Story Beyond Death*, Ann Marie feels her spiritual bond with her husband has only become stronger since the time of his death. She quotes Ira Gershwin *"Deep unspeakable suffering may well be called a baptism, a regeneration, the initiation into a new state."* I can so resonate with this beautiful quote.

I also related to Anne Marie's experience. She writes, *"Love after death is not expected. They tell you to move*

forward, don't wallow in the past; your loved one is gone.
But they are wrong. Love after death is intensely deep and
intimate. I was shocked by its hold on me. I never imagined
our physical and emotional relationship could be deepened
by our spiritual, soul connection in death." For me this is so
true too. I have said often that regardless of not writing
everything down, a story is being written in my head
every day about Dave and me. She later writes of a friend
who lost her husband during the Iraq war. They had only
been together five years, *"It is not the length of time spent*
with your loved one but the depth of love that matters most."

A few years earlier I had bought the book, *Enchanted*
One – The Portal to Love by Sheila Applegate. She was
sharing her book at Healing Inspirations and I found her
comments interesting and uplifting and purchased the
book. The first read through, I knew I was not ready for
it yet and would someday pick it up again. After Dave
passed, I decided to re-read her book, looking for comfort.
In her book, she writes about her beloved husband getting
killed in an accident by some drunken teens. I found

that her level of spirituality had developed well beyond my own. She appeared accepting and forgiving of those who altered her life forever with their careless decision. She speaks of the three years it took her to work through her anger and depression. She then came to her portal of love to understand the deeper meaning of his death that would create more love and peace then she had ever known. Sheila writes:

> *"But beyond that, it was the unfolding of a divine plan that would allow my beloved Twin Flame to serve the Creator in an even greater way than he could have on Earth. It would allow him to walk with me beyond any illusion of separation and expand his love and service to levels I could not even conceive of at the time. So how could I condemn the people or the choices that had created this circumstance? I could not."*

Sometimes, when people lose someone to traumatic death it can perpetuate a deep desire to research the afterlife. I feel that some of our religious faiths dropped the ball by not teaching enough about death. It was always a mystery or area where myths and fear were created. This new understanding of life beyond my experience, of readings and of others' testimonies were beautiful, yet still I question why was I entering into this? There isn't a day that passes where "Why?" isn't asked.

In a segment from *Oprah on Super Soul Sunday*, October 30, 2017, her guest Dr. Weiss discussed the many forms of angels from his book, *Miracles Happen*. Oprah says, *"But the essence of that person, the heart, the love of that person, particularly if you've know them on earth, I find become more powerful because you are infused with that energy and that spirit in a way you never were before."* Dr. Weiss replied, *"Energy does not have boundaries."* I love this because he says that before we are reunited they are with us. Over my lifetime, I was told of my sensitive nature and I thought this was weakness. I now realize this sensitivity is my gift and has opened me to a whole new realm.

I have managed my life over these years always living in the now and able to do anything required, and it took over three years from the anniversary of his death to feel a little less burdened. Over the years I tried Hypnotherapy,

Emotional Freedom Techniques, Emotional Code, Reiki, mediums, and many expensive means to stop the pain. As a person of strong faith, I saw the metaphysical gifts as an extension of a solid faith I live. Prayer is the constant in my life, so that was my main lifeline while waiting to receive peace and understanding. The holistic gifts helped pacify me after a most difficult shock to my system, giving, me a gradual healing but also bringing me closer to understanding Dave and why we are connected.

This past year, I took a few weeks off, escaping to another part of the world to renew and bring some closure upon return. I found peace and solace living in the moment volunteering on one of the Cook Islands in the South Pacific and embraced it. I held the memories but never once was my loss of Dave forgotten or not held with appreciation and respect. As Dave said through a medium, this story is not over yet and he has a close second I will meet.

I do believe Dave and I will see each other again. I do believe there was a deliberate connection to me that I was not asking to happen in this way. I do believe that I would never have spent over three years inspired to write this story for myself if it were not for his presence. The inspiration to share my story came from beyond and the over three years was the necessary time to bring in the answers I could digest, the healing and the decision to release this to publication. It all started by looking at the pictures at the wake and wondering, how did I forget the essence of him? I will have answers for my experience that I believe will validate what I have already learned on this side. I pray for his soul. Every day, I pray for his family as if they were my own. I understand if this story is a turn off for those who never experienced anything like this or if it doesn't fit others' beliefs. My Christian walk has always been an experience revealing to me how much I have yet to learn. Spirituality is a process lest our spiritual growth be stopped. There is so much to learn in Earth's classroom.

Before submitting this for publishing, I went once more to a highly regarded and gifted woman in our local area, Maura the Medium. Dave was aware of my writing and said he was my muse. He most definitely deserves the right to be labeled co-creator – divinely inspiring me through the writing. There were many affirmations in Maura's reading as to what I have believed and heard before of his presence. She was emphatic that this journey would not end but continue into the hereafter. He most definitely wanted me to stop the writing and let it go as the gift it was intended to be in respect and honor of both of us. My releasing this story is just in time for his birthday. I felt that the story — of two people who have been misunderstood quite a bit and who lived not quite in a place that would have made life's journey easier to walk — needed to be told.

Maura said she saw him on a boat. I said that was funny because over the years I have collected pictures of boats that I visualized were where my special someone and I would spend time. She felt that early on I had a higher intuitive ability that was drawing his presence in. Dave told her there was more significance to the pictures.

We truly were two ships passing in the night. We were not intended to continue on this earthly plane but this was far from over.

Since the decision to stop writing and publish, a huge weight was lifted off me. I sense sadness and grief but there is something significantly different. Regardless of my appearance on the outside, this release of my story brought a shift I could feel and has brought an inner peace that I have not had for over 3 years. The release of this story is my gift to Dave and myself.

I am forever grateful for writers I have found who shared their experience, as they have helped me to strengthen my faith each day. Regardless of how much I have described grief and sadness, I am aware these burdens are part of what I live but are not my identity, my life as a whole or my future. I hope and pray this book will bring hope and peace to anyone who has lost a loved one or is afraid of the life beyond. Understanding is the beginning of wisdom.

I was told years ago by Sr. Maureen D'Onofrio that my tears are a form of prayer as tears express something far deeper than words. Tears help fertilize the soul…some call them holy tears. If so, Dave has been blessed with many prayers for his soul's journey. A very appropriate closing thought from Dr. Seuss, *"Sometimes you will never know the value of a moment until it becomes a memory."*

Acknowledgements

First I have to acknowledge the women of Healing Inspirations, a holistic healing and learning center. As I look back over the three years, each practitioner played a part in my journey. The practitioners are Betsy Sams, Michele Love, Deborah DeRusha, Sharon Quinn, Suzanne Masters, Krystal Martin Murphy and Karen Scanlon, editorial consultant.

I also acknowledge the beautiful members of a unique book club, Lorraine Paradise White and her encouraging mentoring practice, Cynde Forst, Kelly Murphy, Michele McLaughlin and Suzanne Masters, who taught me the gift of tapping to release emotions.

Others who shared their experience, wisdom and advice: Denise McKee, Doreena Clifton, Anne Marie Higgins, Sheila Applegate, Lenore Vaccarello, Sr. Maureen D'Onofrio, Lorraine Pagano, Maura the Medium and Hope for the Bereaved.

I am grateful to my dear cousin, Barbara Davis, for her final copy edits. Finally, I extend my gratitude to the OASIS Creative Writing class. If it were not for them I may have never started or finished my story.

All of these people didn't just listen but understood the world of the spirit and some encouraged my healing through writing. As I dealt with death and grief, I came to understand there is a greater inspiration from the beyond motivating this book. I would encourage writing in dealing with pain even if it is a few sentences, a word, anything to release emotions that you do not want stuffed inside you but sent back to the Universe and to God.

CPSIA information can be obtained
at www.ICGtesting.com
Printed in the USA
BVHW07s1949250718
522612BV00011B/793/P